artworld

What Is

IMPRESSIONISM?

by Kate Riggs

CREATIVE EDUCATION · CREATIVE PAPERBACKS

Published by Creative Education and Creative Paperbacks
P.O. Box 227, Mankato, Minnesota 56002
Creative Education and Creative Paperbacks are
imprints of The Creative Company
www.thecreativecompany.us

Design and production by Chelsey Luther
Art direction by Rita Marshall
Printed in the United States of America

Photographs by The Bridgeman Art Library (Edgar Degas, James
Abbott McNeill Whistler), Corbis (Leemage, Berthe Morisot/Francis G.
Mayer), Getty Images (Claude Monet/Buyenlarge/Buyenlarge/Time Life
Pictures, Pierre-Auguste Renoir), Wikimedia Creative Commons (Gustave
Caillebotte/DcoetzeeBot, Edouard Manet/Tungsten, Claude Monet/
DcoetzeeBot, Camille Pissarro, Camille Pissarro/Paris 16, Pierre-Auguste
Renoir/Bwwm)

Library of Congress Cataloging-in-Publication Data
Riggs, Kate.
What is impressionism? / Kate Riggs.
p. cm. — (Art world)
Summary: With prompting questions and historical background, an early
reader comes face to face with famous works of Impressionist art and is
encouraged to identify light and shadow and consider feelings evoked.
Includes bibliographical references and index.
ISBN 978-1-60818-626-6 (hardcover)
ISBN 978-1-62832-224-8 (pbk)
ISBN 978-1-56660-692-9 (eBook)
1. Impressionism (Art)—Juvenile literature. I. Title.

N6465.I4R54 2016
709.03'44—dc23   2015008501

CCSS: RI.1.1, 2, 3, 5, 6, 7; RI.2.1, 2, 3, 5, 6, 7; RI.3.1, 3, 5, 7; RF.1.1; RF.2.3, 4;
RF.3.3

First Edition HC
9 8 7 6 5 4 3 2 1
First Edition PBK
9 8 7 6 5 4 3 2 1

Contents

Color and Light 4

Make an Impression 6

Dawning 8

Friends at Lunch 11

Dancing in the Sunlight 12

At the Ballet 14

Taking to the Streets 16

Impressionism and You 18

Portrait of an Impressionist 21

Glossary 22

Read More Websites 23

Index 24

Colors swirl. Light fades.

Color and Light

What do you see in a painting? If you see a lot of light and soft lines, you may be looking at Impressionism.

Woman with a Parasol—Madame Monet and Her Son (1875), by Claude Monet

5

Make an Impression

An "impression" happens right away.
Impressionists wanted to show how life
changes quickly. They painted outside.

They looked at flowers and sunlight. They looked at people walking down the street.

Left: *The Skiff* (1875), by Pierre-Auguste Renoir; above: *Paris Street; Rainy Day* (1877), by Gustave Caillebotte

Dawning

Impressionism started in France. Claude Monet painted *Impression, Sunrise* in 1872. Boats are in a harbor at sunrise. Everything is dim and gray. But the sun is bright. The lines are blurry and soft.

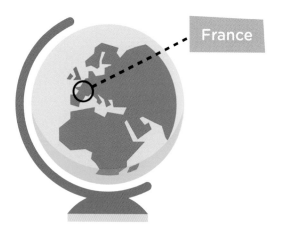

France

Monet's painting gave Impressionism its name.

A group of friends enjoys lunch in Renoir's painting.

Friends at Lunch

How does the light change later in the day? Pierre-Auguste Renoir paints lunchtime light in *Luncheon of the Boating Party* (1881). The light is much brighter!

Dancing in the Sunlight

Renoir liked painting people in real life.
He shows people having fun in *Dance at
the Moulin de la Galette* (1876). Patches of
sunlight shine through the trees.

People in Paris held outdoor dances in the 1870s.

At the Ballet

Renoir and Monet painted outside a lot. But Edgar Degas liked to draw indoors. He loved painting **ballet** dancers. *The Rehearsal* (1874) looks like we are walking into a dance class.

How many dancers can you see in this work?

Taking to the Streets

Impressionists liked to show the same place or person at different times. Camille Pissarro painted a street in Paris. You can see crowds

of people there on a sunny day. What do the people look like at night? They are dark smudges on the sidewalks!

Left: *Boulevard Montmartre* (1897);
above: *Boulevard Montmartre la nuit* (1898)

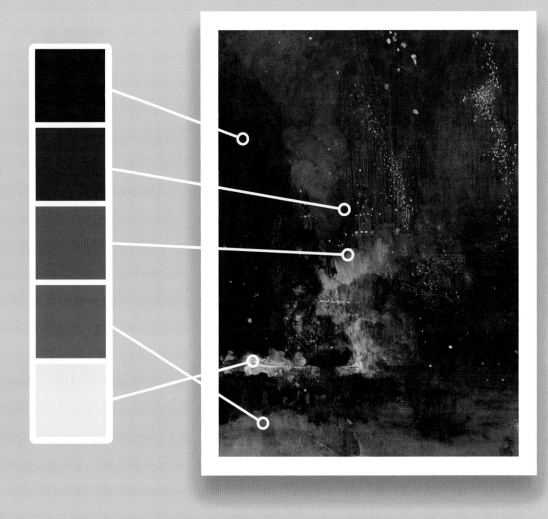

Impressionism and You

How do you feel when you look at Impressionism? What colors do you see? Can you make an impression of your life?

Spot the different colors in this painting by James Abbott McNeill Whistler.

Portrait of an Impressionist

Berthe Morisot was born in France in 1841. Berthe liked painting gardens and landscapes. She painted people inside their homes, too. Berthe's daughter Julie is in many of her paintings.

Left: a picture of Berthe by Edouard Manet; above: *Woman at Her Toilette* (1875/80)

Glossary

ballet—a dance done to music by dancers wearing pointe shoes

harbor—a place on the coast where boats are kept

landscapes—pictures about the countryside

Read More

Anholt, Laurence. *The Magical Garden of Claude Monet*. London: Barron's, 2007.

Cocca-Leffler, Maryann. *Edgar Degas: Paintings That Dance*. New York: Grosset & Dunlap, 2001.

Websites

NGAkids Art Zone
http://www.nga.gov/content/ngaweb/education/kids.html
Make your own art, and learn more about Impressionism at the National Gallery of Art.

Sing-along at the Metropolitan Museum of Art
http://www.metmuseum.org/metmedia/kids-zone/start-with -art/sing-along
Sing along to identify paintings by famous Impressionists.

NOTE: Every effort has been made to ensure that the websites listed above are suitable for children, that they have educational value, and that they contain no inappropriate material. However, because of the nature of the Internet, it is impossible to guarantee that these sites will remain active indefinitely or that their contents will not be altered.

Index

colors **4, 8, 18**

Degas, Edgar **14**

France **8, 16, 21**

light and shadow **4, 5, 8, 11, 12**

Monet, Claude **8, 14**

Morisot, Berthe **21**

painting outside **6, 14**

Pissarro, Camille **16**

Renoir, Pierre-Auguste **11, 12, 14**

subjects **7, 8, 12, 14, 16–17, 21**